"Are You Out There, God?"

Sr. Mary Rose McGeady

Covenant House

DEDICATED
to the 1,000,000
homeless children
who slept on America's streets last year,
scared, cold, hungry, alone
and most of all, desperate to find
someone who cares.

Table of Contents

Introduction

*"Their hearts have
only one question."*

Have you ever asked a question and not wanted to hear the answer?

Homeless kids do this all the time. One they often ask is, "What did I do to deserve this?"

I can't tell you how many times I've heard a homeless girl whisper that question. Or how many times I've seen that question in the haunted eyes of a homeless boy.

But what really tears at my heart is that in most cases, these street kids don't want to hear the answer.

Deep inside, they're sure they already know ... and it's killing them.

They believe the abuse they've suffered, the neglect, the abandonment by their families ... the pain of life alone on the cold and brutal streets ... is all their fault.

And they think that God must not care.

That's why they often ask another question that they don't want to hear the answer to: "Are you out there, God?"

I know the answer to this one. I know God loves these kids — and perhaps loves them the most of all, because they need Him the most.

But telling these kids God loves them isn't enough. I know because I've tried. They can't believe it.

And so I've learned to show them God's love — with a hot meal, a change of clothes, a safe place to sleep, a listening ear ... and a warm hand on a trembling shoulder.

I'm Sister Mary Rose McGeady. For six years now, I've been in charge of the largest crisis center and shelter for homeless kids in the country. It's called Covenant House.

This book, "Are You Out There, God?" contains stories about a few of the hundreds of thousands of kids we've seen at Covenant House in my time here.

There's Nancy, known to our kids as "The Girl in the Hood," who came to Covenant House wracked with such self-loathing and feelings of unworthiness, that she covered her entire head with a red hood and kept it on there, never taking it off for weeks at a time.

And there's the girl who hurtled herself against our rescue van one night, desperately trying to escape a pimp who was trying to kill her (this despicable man had long since murdered her innocence).

Theirs are true stories. Tragic stories. Chilling and graphic stories of life on the streets. And yet, if you read between the lines, you'll find in them something beautiful.

It's the answer to the question, "Are You Out There, God?"

The answer is: "Yes!" God is out there — and

He's also inside each one of these kids, waiting to be revealed.

You see, I have discovered that even in the most desperate child, there is hope. It may be only the very smallest of sparks — impossible to see at first. Finding it often takes time and patience, requiring us to carefully scrape away the overlay of scars, pain, hurt, rejection and suffering to find the hope which abides in every human heart. The child may not even know it's there. But it is. And at Covenant House everyone, from our counselors to our cooks, shelters this tiny spark, feeds it, nurtures it....

I hope you'll take the time to read my book. I hope you'll be as moved and inspired by these strong, courageous kids as I was, day after day. I've told their stories through letters I wrote to my friends over the past few years — friends who share Covenant House's life-saving mission with me.

And I'm hoping that by the end of this book, you will pray for my kids, pray for our mission — and become my friend, too.

Please, help me answer our kids' question — "Are You Out There, God?"

Sister Mary Rose McGeady
June 9, 1996

No stranger I, to death.
He lives with me each day.
He tempts me with my grave,
and hides the price I'll pay.

A poem from
a street kid

Chapter 1

"If they find me, they'll kill me."

"I'm what they call a mule, Sister," the girl said.

"They made me smuggle drugs for them," she said.

"They stuffed cocaine in little plastic bags, and made me swallow them," she said.

She sat in our clinic — her on the edge of a nervous breakdown, me on the edge of my seat, searching for some words that could help Liz bear a lifetime of unbearable pain.

I know what the term "mule" means on the street, but I have never met one so young.

Liz is 14 years old.

"The drug runners made me a drug mule. Me and my friend, Michelle."

"Michelle is dead now," she said. "She was the same age as me."

"That must have been awful," I said.

"It was," she said.

"Michelle and I come from London and we did the New York run. In London, they'd make us swallow bags filled with drugs. Sometimes I didn't even know what was in them.

"A few weeks ago, Michelle and I were waiting to

get picked up when she started to feel real sick. She got worse and worse and then she collapsed on the sidewalk. When the dealers came to pick us up, they made me leave her there.

"I found out that she died on the way to the hospital. A bag burst inside her and the drugs killed her.

"And I'm next, Sister. Sooner or later. I know it. That's why I had to come here. But if they find me, they'll kill me."

"No one's going to kill you, Liz. You're safe here."

"You don't know these people, Sister. They wouldn't think twice about shooting you or anyone else."

For another hour, I went around and around with Liz, trying to convince her she was safe ... trying to convince her she was worth saving.

She told me about her life. How her mother needed money so she put Liz to work with a local pimp. She was 12 years old. Liz shook with disgust and pain when she told me how she was forced to have sex with dozens of perverted men every week.

Then, six months ago, her pimp decided he had a new use for her. He wanted her to carry drugs through customs — to be a drug "mule."

Liz resisted, but her pimp said it wasn't her choice. He owned her, and she had to do what he wanted.

So out of fear, Liz became a mule, part of a rapidly-growing herd of defenseless kids being manipulated and used by the multi-billion dollar drug and sex industry.

These greedy men in their $2,000 designer suits use kids like Liz to smuggle drugs for some unforgivable reasons. Because kids are trustworthy. Because they are innocent looking. In short, because they are kids.

Kids like Liz are being increasingly used to run drugs because they are the perfect "front men" for the crime ... and the best "insurance" that the deal will be completed.

One policeman I talked to recently summed it up: "These kids are the perfect puppets, Sister. They don't raise a lot of suspicion. And they're so young, and so scared, they do exactly what they're told...."

I loathe these drug dealers and pushers. I loathe and despise what they do to kids like Liz. I hate their cruelty and viciousness. I know maybe I should find a place in my heart to forgive them, God, but I can't. I just can't....

"I couldn't take it anymore," Liz said, tears gushing out. "I'm not bad, Sister. I'm really not bad...."

"I know that, Liz," I said. "I know. But, don't worry. I just know we'll be able to help." Somehow, those words made her cry even harder.

Chapter 2

"I got no place to go."

"No thanks, Sister," the tiny voice called out from the shadows. "I'll be OK. Don't worry."

The tiny kid standing in the darkness felt his voice crack, and I knew he was lying.

I caught the lump in my throat, and tried to stay cool.

For several nights, our Covenant House van team had pursued the 10-year-old boy, pulling alongside him to offer help, but never acting so anxious or scared for him that he would pull away.

"Do you need a place to stay — can we help you — will you come with us?" we asked him every night.

"No, I'll be all right," the tiny voice said, trying to act like he meant it.

I could see the longing in his eyes every time he said no. I kept praying to God that he'd change his mind, before it was too late. I knew time was running out for him....

Finally, tonight, the big breakthrough came.

Tonight, when he stepped out of the shadows, his face was black and blue and swollen and dripping tears that he had hidden from us before.

"I'm scared," he finally said. "I got no place to go."

I reached out and hugged him as hard as I could, but he was shaking so hard I couldn't get a good grip. Before I could jump out of the van, he was already on the pavement, sobbing.

He was still crying when we finally got him into a bed at our crisis center.

We don't even know his name. He's been too tired and embarrassed and proud to give it to us.

I can't get him out of my mind this morning. I wonder what he's thinking now, if he's dreaming. I wonder if he's *ever* for even one day lived a life that you or I would want to live? Even for one day....

I already imagine what he'll say to me the first time we talk.

"Hi, my name is ____," he'll say. "I'm sorry I put you through all this trouble," he'll say. "This is really embarrassing ending up like this." (You'd be amazed how many of our kids are overwhelmed with embarrassment when they come to our shelter. For all their hurt, and pain and incredible sorrow, street kids are most scared of being looked down on. Of smelling bad, and looking dirty. As if being 15 and homeless and unwanted is all their fault....)

"I ... I don't have any place to go, Sister," the boy will then tell me. "I wish I did, but my (fill in the blank ... stepmother, father, parents ...) beat me, and I couldn't live there anymore.

"No one loves me," the boy will say.

"I tried to survive on the streets, Sister, I really did. But I was too tired and too hungry...."

And then, in the quiet of tonight, this little kid who is still so tired he can barely keep his eyes open, and so hurt and lonely he can't remember the last time anyone hugged him (if anyone has *ever* hugged him), will break down again and cry.

I will let him know that we truly care for him, and that he can stay with us as long as he likes, and that yes, we truly do love him.

And, like every Covenant House kid, he will look at me with tear-filled eyes, half disbelieving and half wondering, and he'll say, "Thanks, Sister. Thanks for taking me in."

And I will thank God at that moment for you.

Chapter 3

"I'm glad the pimps don't like us...."

"Help! Help me! Please help me!"

She came sprinting out of the darkness, as fast as her legs could carry her, and literally jumped on the running board of our van.

She kept banging on the window — pounding, pounding — to get our attention. Her eyes were overflowing with fear.

For a split second, we were scared to death she'd fall off and kill herself.

Our driver slammed on the brakes, and grabbed for the door to let her in.

"No, no, please don't stop here. My man is watching ... he'll see me get in. He'll know where I am. Go over to that alleyway over there. I'll get in then when he can't see me. He'll never know where I went...."

Before we could convince her to jump in, she leapt off the van, and raced off to a different alleyway. She was running, swerving, dodging across the dark street, doing all she could to confuse whoever it was — whatever it was — that was chasing her.

We stepped on the gas, and raced our van to the alleyway she had asked us to go to. Our driver turned off the van and the headlights, and waited in the darkness.

Seconds later, the girl came running toward the van, from another direction. In an effort to fool her pimp, she had run completely around the block.

She was only about 30 yards from our van and safety. Then it happened.

A huge car came screeching around the corner, its headlights off in the darkness, and aimed itself directly at our van.

Sheila, our van driver, spotted the car at the last minute, turned the key and slammed on the gas. The car barely missed ramming our van.

Then it sped off, and headed right for the girl.

Although it was impossible to really see much in the darkness of midnight, it was clear that the girl was very, very young. Fifteen at the most, maybe even twelve or thirteen.

She raced across the street, with the car right behind her. The car careened over the median strip, over curbs, like a hungry shark after its prey.

Finally, it pulled alongside the girl. A man jumped out, grabbed the child by the throat and started beating her.

And then he picked her up, and threw her into the car.

Our van raced after the car as fast as we could. Sheila took the license plate number, and telephoned it into the police.

But they said there was nothing we could do.

The car got away. Our van hasn't seen the girl for

a week. We're really worried if we'll ever see her again.

I wish I could tell you that this was some sickening scene I saw from some Grade B movie, filled with make-believe actors on a make-believe streetcorner.

But I can't. *Every single word of this story is true!*

I can't get this girl out of my mind. I keep thinking about her every minute. She was so close to my outstretched hands, so close to being saved. But she ended up in the scummy hands of her pimp, a sick man driving a big car, sleazing through life at the expense of little girls.

I hope you'll excuse the brutality of my letter this month. This is not the letter I had planned to write!

I was going to write you about a beautiful 16-year-old girl named Donna, one of our newest walking, talking, smiling success stories. I walked on air for two whole days after I met Donna, her story was so beautiful. I really wanted to tell you about her this month.

But then I met this girl running toward our van. I can't get her out of my mind. I had to tell you about her.

I'm having a little trouble finding the words I need to say. I guess I feel the need to stress something I'm sure you know already. Covenant House is not "make believe." Not every ending is a "happy ending" for our kids.

In trying and crying and sweating to save the lives of homeless kids, we don't always succeed.

I think if I had to really sum up what we are, we're just a good shelter for kids that is deliberately placed in the midst of a sometimes horrible, dangerous world ... right where God wants us to be.

Our volunteers and staff — wonderful people like Sheila driving the van — put themselves at risk every day. (Not long ago, the back window of our van was shattered by gunfire.)

A pimp — angry because we were trying to "steal" one of his girls — shot at our van. Other pimps have thrown rocks at us, knives at us ... everything.

But do you know what? I'm proud the pimps don't like us. Because none of us here care much for them either. I don't like them. And I'm going to keep making sure we do everything in our power to stop them.

We're never going to turn our backs on these lost children.

Dear God,
I just want someone to love me, someone to talk to
when I need to talk. Someone to cry on when I
need to cry. Most of all someone to love me and
walk as far as they wish through my life. Amen.

A prayer written
by a kid in our
Covenant House chapel

Chapter 4

"We all live in a box," he said.

"We all live in a box," the biggest kid said.

"A what?" I said.

"A box," he said.

"How many of you live in it?" I said.

"All six of us," he said.

"Six of you, in the same box?" I said.

"Well, yeah," the oldest boy said, a little embarrassed at the thought. "I mean, it's a big box."

"Yeah, Sister," the littlest one said. "It is pretty big, Sister."

"It really concerns me that you are outside," I said. "Why aren't you home?" I said (although I already knew the answer).

"I don't got a home," the littlest kid said. "My father ... my father beat me," he said. "I had to run ... I was really afraid he was going to kill me," he said.

"Same with me," the middle kid said. "Me too," the big one said. "There ain't no such thing as home," a fourth kid said. "My mom and dad beat me too," another kid said.

The six kids huddled closer together and stared at me, trying not to look too ashamed or embarrassed about how they looked and how they sounded.

They were dirty, and bedraggled, and unkempt and

dressed in rags — and they were infinitely beautiful. Under all the filth and insecurity, I could see six great children.

Six beautiful kids who lived inside a box. I wanted to hug them all.

"It's really not a bad box," the youngest (who looked about 11 or 12) mumbled again. I could tell he felt hurt, and desperately needed my approval.

"I'm sure you make it as good as it ever could be," I smiled back, and patted his little back.

"Yeah, it's a big cement box," one of the middle kids said. "It has some kind of transformer inside, which is great 'cause it gives off heat and keeps us warm at night. This past winter, that really came in handy," he said.

"It really helped in the winter," the little one chimed in again. "Yeah, it really did." His eyes were so beautiful and pure I felt like I was going to cry.

"Do you think I could see this box?" I asked. "I mean, is that OK?"

The kids looked at each other, waiting for the oldest boy to make the decision. But the youngest couldn't wait. "Sure, Sister," he said. "It's not far from here."

When we got there, the kids scrambled over a chain link fence surrounding a sort of concrete cavern. I didn't even try to follow them. The idea of a 65-year-old nun trying to climb a fence was just too ridiculous.

The kids stood in front of their box beaming like elementary school kids showing their teacher an art project.

"It's great," the biggest kid said. He was obviously the leader. "It's dry and warm and even has a fence for protection. So don't worry about us," he said. The others nodded.

I wanted to point out to him how quickly he had climbed that fence and how little protection it really was. But it was the "Don't worry about us" that really got to me.

"You know," I said, "we've got a great place for you to stay tonight, if you don't want to sleep in this box. We've got warm, clean beds, and good food, and clean clothes, and you can take a hot shower. Would you like to come back to our shelter with me?" I said.

I was trying to act cool, because I didn't want them to see how scared and worried I was for them, because that would only make them more scared and worried.

For their part, they tried to act like they didn't hear me. The moment I invited them in, all eyes dropped to the ground, not ready to trust anyone yet, in a world they already knew could never be trusted.

"Well, thanks, but not now," the oldest finally said. "We got it all figured out," he said. "We're like a family. We all take care of each other."

I resisted the temptation to lecture them about their dream world. They probably wouldn't listen ... and they'll learn soon enough on their own.

I just hope they're still alive enough to learn.

I wanted to yell. "YOU CALL THIS A FAMILY! A FAMILY IS SUPPOSED TO PROTECT KIDS

AND HELP THEM PREPARE FOR LIFE!

"NOT ONE OF YOU IS OVER 18. YOU DON'T KNOW ANYTHING ABOUT LIFE YET! BUT YOU'RE GOING TO LEARN.

"YOU'RE GOING TO LEARN ABOUT PIMPS AND PUSHERS. YOU'RE GOING TO LEARN ABOUT PNEUMONIA — AND EVEN WORSE DISEASES. YOU'RE GOING TO LEARN ABOUT HUNGER AND HOW QUICKLY YOU CAN DIE. HAVE YOU THOUGHT ABOUT THAT?

"HAVE YOU THOUGHT ABOUT THE REST OF YOUR LIVES? DO YOU REALLY WANT TO LIVE IN A CEMENT BOX FOREVER? AND IF NOT, HOW WILL YOU EVER GET OUT OF HERE?

"I'LL TELL YOU HOW, BECAUSE THERE ARE ONLY THREE WAYS. DRUGS, PROSTITUTION ... OR DEATH.

"THAT'S IT, KIDS. THAT'S YOUR FUTURE."

I didn't say any of those things. I looked at those bright, hopeful — and hopelessly naive — faces and I asked God to watch over them. I'm sure He will....

"GOD! YOU BETTER WATCH OVER THESE KIDS! AND YOU BETTER SEND THEM TO US BEFORE IT'S TOO LATE!" I prayed.

In the end, I gave the kids sandwiches, some clothes ... and I gave them each a Covenant House card. I promised them we'd be ready whenever they need us.

"Thanks anyway," they said.

Please don't hold it against these kids that they are

so naive. They are just so glad to escape from abusive home lives, and they're full of the wonderful optimism of youth.

Unfortunately, they will soon learn what a dangerous, ugly, dehumanizing place the streets are. I've been praying for them ever since I left them. (By the way, because a bunch of the kids were underage, we contacted the authorities to let them know where they were — I want every available set of eyes looking after these kids!)

Chapter 5

"How long have you been living in this car?"
I asked. "Nine months," he said.

"I'm not really homeless, Sister," the scraggly kid said. "I'm doing OK. I mean, it's not like I'm sleeping on the sidewalk. I have a home. Right here. See?"

Bobby turned and pointed to the home he lived in — an abandoned, beaten up wreck of a car. I had to catch my breath when I saw it. The car was so dirty, so rusted, with broken windows, I couldn't imagine a kid sleeping inside it for one night, let alone calling it home.

"You live in there," I said, my voice rising to form a question. "Well ... yeah," he said, beginning to feel a little embarrassed. "It's not that bad. Really, it's pretty good."

"How long have you been living in this car?" I asked.

"Nine months," he said.

"Through all of last winter?" I asked.

"Yeah," he said, visibly shaking for a second while a shiver ran down his spine. "For some of the really, really cold nights I slept in the subway," he said. "But most of the time ... it wasn't really that bad," he said.

The last sentence crept out of his mouth a lot slower than the others. I could tell he was forcing himself to pry the words out one at a time, words that sounded good, and brave and courageous. He desperately wanted to, needed to, sound like he was happy. Amidst all the wreckage around him, from the old car to the rags he was wearing, he desperately grabbed onto all the dignity he had left inside. It was all he had left....

"I'd like to help you," I said. "I work at a place called Covenant House," I said.

"I've heard of it," he said. "It's a place for kids who don't have any place to go," he said. "I'm not one of them," he said. "I'm doing OK," he said, trying to sound brave again.

"Well, even so, we'd love to help you," I said. "We've got a nice clean shelter, with clean beds, and clothes, and you can get some good food and take a hot shower and get some help," I said.

His eyes became filled with a faraway look, as if the simple things I had mentioned — a place to sleep, clothes, food, a shower — were treasures from a magical kingdom far away. He couldn't bring himself to say yes. But his eyes were telling me he desperately wanted to come back with me.

"How did you end up on the street," I asked.

"Well ... my family broke up last summer," he said. "My mom and dad ... Dad ran away to another town, and Mom kind of freaked out and she just said she was going away too. 'You're seventeen, Bobby,' she said. 'I think you're ready to go out on your own.' "

"I'm so sorry," I said. "Yeah," his eyes said.

"What happened after that," I said.

"Well, I didn't know what to do," he said. "I don't have any other family. I tried sleeping at some friends' houses, but that didn't last long. So I spent a couple nights on the street. Then I found this car. It was the end of summer, it was comfortable ... so I decided to live in here.

"Ever since then, I just kind of sleep in this car at night, and use the showers at school."

"You still go to school?" I asked.

"Well, yeah," he said.

"How do you study?" I said. I had a million other questions, but that seemed like the most logical place to start.

"I study at work," he said. "When my shift is done, I hang around until closing time. I don't have any lights here in the car. That's the only problem," he said.

"Where do you work?"

"At a hamburger place," he said. "It's good 'cause I get free meals, too. I've been working there for about six months."

"And then, you come back to the car after work," I said.

"Yeah," he said. He couldn't hide the sadness in his voice this time. The memories of all those nights in the car were really starting to get to him.

"Bobby, do you feel safe sleeping in this car?" I asked.

He looked at me with one of those looks you get from a teenage kid, a look that said, "C'mon, what do you think? Feel safe? Sleeping alone in the city? In an abandoned car with broken windows?"

"Not really," he said. "I mean, it's pretty comfortable, but I don't sleep a lot. Noises wake me up at night. It can be pretty rough out here," he said.

"Bobby, could you do me a big favor," I said.

"Could you try Covenant House out tonight? Just this one night? I think you'd really like it there," I said.

To my surprise and complete joy, he finally let his guard down. "Well ... maybe for a night," he said. "I could use a bathroom," he said. "But I got to come back," he said. "I'm really OK."

I ushered Bobby over to my car. (By the way, it was purely providential I ran into Bobby tonight. I didn't even know a kid lived in that abandoned car. I had just decided to go for a drive to see what was new around the city, and I had seen him on the corner, dressed in rags, looking like a kid who didn't have a place to go, and I had pulled over to talk to with him....)

All the way back to Covenant House, Bobby just sat there, quiet. I tried to start a conversation, but he was all alone in his own thoughts. I think maybe he was wondering if this was a good idea, or maybe he was wondering how a 17-year-old kid like him ends up on the street all alone, sleeping in an abandoned car for nine months.

I'd like to think maybe he was just alone in his dreams, wondering if tonight was the night his luck and life was finally going to change. That's what I was thinking while I drove and prayed....

Help Me

Help me, Dear Lord
    as I travel towards You.
There are many detours
    which will try to distract
    me away from You.
Help me as I travel my path
    to cherish the parents You gave me.
Help me to do my best in all my endeavors
    whether I may win or lose.
Help me never to lose hope
    though there may be difficult times.
Help me to choose good friends.
Help me to choose the right mate,
    so that I may have a happy family someday.
Help me, though I may fall,
    to continue on my journey towards You.
Help me, Dear Lord.
I want so much to be with You. Amen.

                    Written by a
                    Covenant House kid

Chapter 6

"God, I can't believe they did this to me!"

The cab hurtled down 10th Avenue, careened onto a sidewalk on 41st, and then screeched to a dead stop in front of our shelter.

"I got a kid here," the cab driver blurted out, leaping onto the sidewalk. "I got a kid here ... geez, she's in really bad shape ... she gave me 20 bucks to bring her here. Geeeeez, look at her ... she's just a kid."

Even though the cabby was yelling at the top of his lungs, we could barely hear him. The screaming in the back seat was so loud.

From the sidewalk, in the eerie 2:00 A.M. blackness, we couldn't see the girl in the back seat. Simultaneously enraged, devastated and terrified, she had curled herself into a tightly-wound ball and hidden herself on the floor of the cab.

"I can't believe they did this to me," she kept screeching at the top of her voice. "God, I can't believe they did this to me!"

When our counselors were finally able to coax her out of the back seat, we carried her safely inside.

Fresh bruises covered every inch of her legs.

The kid looked barely 15 years old.

For the next three hours, she did all she could, as

loudly as she could, to tell the world how much she hurt inside. Once, for five minutes, she stopped screaming and crying long enough to take a deep breath, but it was only a temporary reprieve for her and for us. It wasn't until daylight broke over the shelter that she fell into sleep.

For the next 12 hours she slept, tossing and turning. Finally, early the next afternoon, the girl pried her eyes open, looked around and began again to cry.

"I can't believe they did this to me," she kept sobbing into her pillow. "I can't believe anyone could be that cruel...."

I reached out and grabbed her hand, told her it was all right to cry. "You're safe now," I told her. "We want to help you," I said. "We're so sorry," I said.

She looked up at me, dripping in tears, biting her top lip as hard as she could to keep it all inside. "I'm so scared," she said, "I'm so scared."

"We'll take care of you," I said. "Can you tell us what happened?"

"I'm ... I'm too ashamed to tell you," the little girl said. "I ... I don't think you'll like me if I tell you."

"Try me," I smiled. I was beginning to feel a little scared.

"I'm ... I'm a prostitute," she said. The tears were gushing out faster than ever.

"I mean ... I don't want to do that ... I hate it ... I hate it. But I don't have any choice," she said. "My boyfriend says he'll kill me if I don't stay on the street....

"He said he'd kill me," she said.

"What happened last night?" I asked as gently as I could.

"I was on the street ... I had to make extra money tonight ... he was screaming at me as loud as he could ... even though I'd been beat up the night before....

"A cab pulled up ... a man asked me to get in ... he said he'd give me $20 if I did something with him in the cab. I ... needed the money ... I...." For the next five minutes the little girl lay in the bed writhing in tears, sobbing uncontrollably, choking out of breath, watching the horror replay in her head again and again. All I could do was pat her on her back and say how sorry I was. It hardly seemed enough....

"You don't have to go on," I told her. "I understand," I said. "I understand."

"I want to tell you the rest ... I need to tell you what happened," she said.

"I ... did things with the man, while the cab driver drove around. I took the $20 and just jumped out of the cab. I couldn't wait to get away from there.

"As I got out of the car I knew I couldn't do it anymore. I was sick and angry ... and I hurt all over. So, I jumped in another cab, gave the cab driver the $20 and said take me to Covenant House. I couldn't take it anymore....

"I can't take it anymore. I can't believe my boyfriend made me do this. He said he cared about me," she screamed.

For the past 48 hours we've hovered over the little

girl, keeping watch, protecting her from the hate she
feels for herself. In dribs and drabs, between the
round-the-clock tears, we've been able to piece together her story.

Her name is Melissa. She's 16 years old. She's
from Nebraska. Three years ago, after a terrible fight
with her mother, she packed $327 and some clothes
into a backpack and ran away with a much-older
"boyfriend."

For the past three years, she's been under the
watchful eye of "Sweetpea," a very grimy excuse for a
human being who plies the sexual trade on the
Minnesota Strip. Mr. Sweetpea is about to hear from
us....

As for Melissa and her parents? Melissa promises
us she's going to call tomorrow (we're giving her a few
days to work up the courage). Until then, all of us are
saying extra prayers hoping for the best. Dear God,
she is only a 16-year-old girl. She desperately needs
her family right now....

Run Away

Scared and cold,
first night on the streets
Your body hurts
from your head to your feet

You miss school,
not the work — it's the friends
Thinking what you'll say
when they ask
where you've been

Gotta dollar-fifty,
every penny gotta spend
Make a wrong move ... Boom —
your life comes to an end.

> *Daniel, 16,*
> *a kid on the street*

Chapter 7

"She said those other kids were worth more than me."

He walked right up to me, and launched into it without any preambles. He was 16 years old, and he was a little desperate and very tired, so he decided to get right to the point.

"Sister, how much do you get paid to take care of me?" he asked.

"I mean, how much does the state give you. Do they give you a lot?"

I could tell by Ricky's face there was something in this question much deeper than a curiosity about the finances of Covenant House. It isn't often a 16-year-old gets curious about who pays for the food and rent.

"Why do you want to know, Ricky?"

"Well, it's just ... I was just wondering."

"Are you worried about something?"

"Well, I figured that if you were getting paid by the state to take care of me, then you'd probably keep me around.

"I mean, you'd have to keep me around to get the money, right?" He bit off the word "have" for extra emphasis.

How on earth do these kids become so jaded so fast?

When Ricky walked in here yesterday, we didn't ask him a lot of questions about his past. We wanted to make sure he felt welcome. He told us he was 16 and that he had been on the streets for six months ... ever since his mother threw him out of the house.

He was so exhausted when he walked in that he could barely keep his eyes open. He said he had a hard time sleeping on the streets because he was scared all the time. He said there were very scary people on the streets.

He just woke up from his safe bed at Covenant House a little while ago, after sleeping for almost 24 hours.

"Ricky, money has nothing to do with it. I would want you here if I didn't have a penny in the world. We love you. Now, why did you ask that question?"

"Well ... that's what my mother said when she threw me out. She said she got money from the state for the foster children she took in and if I was gone she could take on one more foster child.

"So she told me to get out. She said she wasn't making any money on me. I'm her son! She said those other kids were worth more than me. She told *me* to get out, Sister!"

Ricky looked up at me, lost in his words. Tears rolled down his face. "Can you believe that, Sister," he kept saying. "Can you believe that?"

I reached out for him, and hugged him for a minute. I could believe it.... Tragically, I hear stories like this all too often. But it doesn't make Ricky's story any easier to accept....

Answers? Solutions? I don't have any.

I wish I did, but I don't. Because of the spiraling breakdown of the American family, more and more kids are freefalling alone, without the safety net of a place to call home. Because of massive budget cuts, programs to help these kids are becoming increasingly invisible. (When budgets get cut, children's programs are traditionally cut to bits. Kids don't march, they don't vote, they don't send money to political campaigns.)

And while the need grows and the "means" shrink, an incredibly dedicated, well-meaning but shrinking army of overworked, underappreciated social workers are doing their best to find a place for these kids.

Somehow, amidst all the good intentions, kids become little living and breathing commodities. Some slip through the cracks. Some, like Ricky, are literally pushed out their front door, and told to make it on their own. It's terrible, it's wrong and it hurts.

And once again, Covenant House stands as the last stop at the end of the dead-end street, ready to pick up the pieces.

I really didn't know how to answer Ricky's question. So I gave him the only answer I could.

"Ricky, we'll always be here for you, no matter what. There is no one more valuable than you in the entire world. You are priceless. I know that, and I'll never forget it. You don't have to worry now."

I think I caught him a little by surprise. "Thanks,

Sister," he said. "You mean it?" he said. "That's really nice," he said.

"Our pleasure," I said. I saw Ricky again about an hour ago, and he ducked around a corner. I think he's still afraid we might change our mind and tell him it's time to leave.

I'll make sure I give him more reassurance tomorrow. Until then, thanks for praying for him, if you can. We never, ever stop thanking God you found us.

I do not consider myself to be a follower,
just a lonely deserted soul in a barbaric city,
who walks his own treacherous path in life.

Written by Brian,
after six months alone
on the street

Chapter 8

"I can't do this for my mother anymore."

The 10-year-old boy came running into our crisis shelter this morning — frantic — scared out of his mind.

"I can't do it anymore," he said to Mattie at our front desk. "I just can't do this for my mother anymore."

At that moment, he reached into his pockets and placed 22 vials of crack and a gun on the shelf. The vials have a street value of $25 a piece. The gun was a 9 millimeter Uzi.

The little boy was crying.

"Please help me," he kept saying. "I just can't do this for my mother anymore...."

You're going to have a hard time believing this letter. What I need to tell you is almost too bizarre and implausible to believe.

It concerns something very new and very scary that we've seen happening out on the streets. *It's very, very important that you know about it....*

These last few months, our crisis team counselors have become increasingly alarmed about a new phenomenon running into our shelter — an exploding population of homeless *girls and boys who've been forced to run drugs for their parents.*

I'm sure you realize that there have always been scattered cases of this reprehensible activity before.

But now — this year, this month — the number of little kids forced to run drugs has begun to skyrocket! What had been a small trickle, has grown into a small stream — a stream of utterly defenseless, totally innocent kids like this 10-year-old boy who are over their heads and drowning on America's streets.

More and more, these little children are ending up on our doorstep because they've been asked to deal drugs by their parents ... and they're too terrified to do it anymore.

These parents use their children to run drugs because the kids are trustworthy, and innocent looking, and resourceful and yes, free of charge. But most of all, these kids are being used to run drugs, because they are the perfect "front man" for the crime ... and the best "insurance" that the deal will be completed.

"It's not likely that a drug dealer will shoot a 10-year-old boy, and steal the money," one policeman told me. "Kids that age just don't get shot at much. But it's not impossible either...."

These little kids are, in many ways, the poorest of the poor at Covenant House. They not only must somehow struggle to survive in a world without love and security. They must carry the incredible extra burden of breaking laws ... running drugs ... being insidiously used and wasted by parents who no longer care about them.

They come to us for a very simple reason: they have no other place to go. There is no "Dickens-like," romantic aura surrounding them. They are hungry, and dirty, and many times dressed in tattered clothes. If you met them you'd be overwhelmed by how very, very terrified they are. And how very tiny and brave, too.

And they are still just little kids.

Please, please understand that these are not bad kids. It's very important you understand this. They are simply innocent kids placed in a situation — a nightmare, an unreal world — that has become the only world they know.

The little boy said it best, when Mattie asked him why he was carrying a 9 millimeter Uzi....

"I have to," he said.

"It comes with my job," he said.

"I sell drugs," he said.

What would you and I do if we were placed in his shoes? I mean, if I were 10 years old, and running "errands" for my mother was the only life I knew — the only life I knew! — would I know enough to escape? Could I? I really don't know the answer to that. I just don't....

I *do* know that we must do absolutely everything we can to care for this kid, and the hundreds of others like him. Now that God has brought him to us, we are going to do all we can to find this child a good home. A place where kids are loved and wanted and cared for. A place every kid should know in his or her lifetime. I've made an absolute promise to him....

Chapter 9

"I ain't got no one," she said.

She came to our shelter for the first time almost five years ago, one of the first Covenant House kids I ever met.

From the second I saw her, I knew she was one of those kids who might not make it. Everything about her, from her tattered clothes to her slumping posture, seemed worn down. Tired. Beaten. Her eyes were two of the oldest eyes I've ever seen on a kid, smeared with pain and sadness. A smell of desperation literally clung to her clothes. I can still see her standing there....

"Hi, I'm Jessica," she mumbled that first time we met.

"I got no place to go ... can I stay here, maybe?" she said.

"I just need to rest for a couple of days," she said.

She was 13 years old.

When she wasn't sleeping during that first visit (and she slept 18 hours that first day — most kids coming down from drugs do), we showered her with as much love and attention as we could.

Getting her clean was a full-time job in itself. It took her 30 minutes to shower away the layers of grime than first day. Picking out pants, and a shirt and sneakers in our clothing room consumed even more time.

"I can't remember the last time I wore a pair of clean clothes," I remember her telling me. "They feel a little funny on me," she said. "I think I'll get used to it, though." A brave staff member neatly piled her old clothes, and dropped them in the trash outside.

My conversations with her? During that first visit they unwound like a springtime of disappointing weather. Every time I sensed she might open up, and I'd be able to break through to her, she would withdraw from me. The only nuggets of information she gave out were dealt to me at her pace, and on her time.

What she shared with me was enough to scare us all to death.

"I've been on the street for two years," she said.

"I ain't got no parents. They left when I was 11," she said.

"I ain't got no one. But I can take care of myself, no problem."

For a couple of days we all loved, consoled and comforted her.

Then, one night, she just left.

During those next few months, I couldn't get her out of my mind. I wondered where she was, how she could survive, and did anyone out there care if she lived or died (the toughest part was knowing that no one "out there" did).

Then, out of the blue, she came back — impossibly dirty again, infinitely alone, obviously strung out and desperate for help.

We welcomed her inside. We fed her. We cleaned her up. And the next day, she left. Again.

It's been that way with Jessica for five years now.

Every few months, just when all of us have given her up for dead, Jessica comes back to us. Looking a little older than before, a little dirtier, a little more scared and alone. I've tried everything to get her to stay, but it's no use.

She *can't* stay with us. There's something inside of her now that simply won't let her stay with us.

It's not that she isn't good and decent, because Jessica is those things. It's just that the drugs and the lure of the street have swallowed Jessica whole, and become her.

As awful as it must feel for her to sleep in dumpsters and alleyways, the street has become Jessica's entire life — her home, her friend, her refuge ... her everything.

Trust in Covenant House? Sure, Jessica can do that for a couple of days, a couple of times a year. But something inside her tells Jessica she can't — she won't — she mustn't — get too close to anyone. (By the way, because Jessica was so young when she first came to Covenant House, we contacted the authorities to let them know she was with us. But Jessica always managed to leave Covenant House right before they got to meet her. She wouldn't trust *anyone*.)

To you and me, this distrust in people sounds strange. But to a girl who's been beaten and abused and abandoned by her parents (as Jessica was), her lack of faith in us is easy to understand.

Wouldn't you or I probably feel the same way?

Earlier this morning, Jessica came to us again.

It had been three months since I last saw her, and she looked awful. The youthful glow that somehow managed to cut through the layers of grime five years ago, is gone now. Her eyes, once tinged with a faint glow of hope, have long since gone blank.

She is alive, in the sense that she is still breathing in and out.

But she is barely alive. I'm really afraid this might be the last time I ever see her again (but I'm never, ever going to give up hope we will save her. Ever!).

"Hi," I said to her when she walked in this morning.

"I'm really glad to see you again," I said.

"Maybe you can stay with us awhile this time," I said, knowing the answer would probably be no.

"Yeah, maybe this time, Sister," she said. "Thanks," she said.

I'm not sure if even Jessica knows whether she'll find the faith to stay with us longer this time. I *do* know that her "thanks" are real. As tired and beaten as she always is when she comes to Covenant House, she never, ever forgets to say "thank you." Ever....

We'll of course love her these next few days, because she is totally deserving of all the love we can muster. The street may own her, but a part of her is ours too. And as long as she is with us, and as long as there is a loving and caring God, there is still hope for

Jessica. I know there is still hope....

I guess I'm stubborn (and I know I'm a natural-born optimist), but I'm never, ever going to give up on us saving Jessica. I mean, when all is said and done, Covenant House is all about hope ... hope that every kid, no matter how bad the circumstances, no matter how great the odds, will find a way to escape their horror on the street, and find a way to a long and fulfilling life.

Maybe you could join me in saying a prayer for her tonight? Please. I know you'd love her if you met her. She really, really is a beautiful kid. She really is....

Chapter 10

"My boyfriend beats me up sometimes if I don't do what he tells me."

She stood on the curb looking scared and lonely and uncomfortable in a skimpy halter top and bright red lipstick.

It was two in the morning. A chilly breeze whipped up the street and seemed to make her shiver. She was just a child.

We pulled our Covenant House van up to the curb, and rolled down the window.

"Hi, what's your name?"

"Janice," she said hesitantly as if she really had to think about her answer.

"Why don't you hop in, Janice? We've got some lemonade and sandwiches. We can talk. You hungry?"

"Yeah, kind of. But not really. I mean, like, I really gotta go. I can't talk now. Maybe later. Will you be back around in a couple hours?"

She glanced nervously up and down the street at the passing cars. We could tell she was dying to jump in, but she was scared. Really scared. The seconds ticked away....

"OK," she finally said. "But only for a minute or two then I gotta go. My boyfriend is gonna be really mad if he finds out I'm doin' this." She climbed in and sat down stiffly across from me.

"Your boyfriend?"

"Yeah, he told me he doesn't want me talking to you guys. So I can't stay long. Can I have a sandwich, too? I'm really hungry."

"Sure, but why do you call him your boyfriend if he lets you walk the street at night? Do you mean your pimp?"

"Oh, no, he's not a pimp, he's my boyfriend," she insisted with dead serious sincerity. "He loves me. He really does. He buys me a lot of nice things."

After a few weeks on the van, you know when a kid is telling you something to convince you ... or telling you something to convince herself. In Janice's case, her fingers gave her away.

All the time she spoke, she couldn't stop twisting the cheap-looking ring on her index finger. It was as if she was trying to control herself ... to lock herself in ... to stop her from saying something that might get her in trouble.

Finally though, she looked up. And she started to sob.

"I ... I'm scared, I'm really scared. Do you think you can help me? My boyfriend beats me up sometimes if I don't do what he tells me. I think ... I think I'm pregnant. Oh God, what am I gonna do?"

We sat there for 20 minutes as Janice's story tumbled out in a torrent of confusion and tears.

She was from Iowa. She'd run away from home

after a bad argument with her parents. She'd met her "boyfriend" at the bus station and he promised to take care of her.

But after a few weeks he demanded Janice pay him back for his favors.

"How old are you, Janice," we asked, trying to guess what she would say. She looked maybe seventeen. But the streets can do that to a kid — make them look a lot older than they really are. We waited as she peered out the van window....

"Fourteen," she said, as a steady stream of tears ran down her cheeks. "I've wanted to quit doing this for a long time. But I didn't know how, or where to go. Then I saw your van tonight. I'd heard about it from some of the other girls. I thought maybe you could help. I was afraid to talk to you. I'm really scared my boyfriend's going to find out I'm here and...." her voice trailed off as she quietly sobbed.

"Can we take you back to Covenant House, Janice? We can help you get out of this mess. We'll go right now if you want. We really don't want to see you go out there now that you've come this far. You've been really brave, you know...."

Janice didn't say a word. Finally, she looked at us and nodded her head with what seemed to be a mixture of relief and dread ... and the van pulled away from the curb and headed back to Covenant House.

As it turned out, Janice was four months pregnant.

And she was even more scared than we realized at first. During her time at Covenant House, she refused to set foot outside even with one of our staff to get some fresh air. She was petrified her "boyfriend" would see her and take her back.

Pimps have a lot to lose if their girls leave them. A typical young prostitute like Janice is worth thousands and thousands of dollars a year to her pimp.

But today the only thing Janice is trying to earn is a new sense of self-respect back home in Iowa. We put her on a plane just a few days after we picked her up off that street.

I hope and pray that Janice is going to make it. But the sad thing is, for every kid like Janice who is rescued off the city streets, there are ten others out there who'll never get the help they need. Each year close to one million kids sleep on the street! 1,000,000! And many of them — too many of them — are dying out there!

If

If all lips spoke the truth,
All pride was cast aside,
Greed was packed and stored away,
And jealousy subside.
If love could rule the universe,
Kindness was sown to every race,
Then one could glance into a mirror
And view God in his face....

Written by a 16-year-old
girl on the street

Chapter 11

*"I'm a little short of cash
today," he told me. "I need you to
go out and earn your keep
before I make you a star," he said.*

WE DID IT! One of America's slimiest, rottenest pimps is sitting in a New York courthouse as I write you, waiting to be sent to jail.

And it's all because of one incredibly-heroic Covenant House kid, and friends like you.

Please read every word of this story. It's going to make you feel great.

It all began in Chicago a few months back, when Cindy, a 17-year-old kid, met "Slim" at a party. "He didn't look like a rotten pimp at all when I first met him," Cindy said. "He was dressed real nice, and he was real friendly, and he had these fancy business cards. He said he was a big music promoter who made videos for groups like _____ and _____ (your kids would recognize the names).

"He said he liked the way I danced. He said he could make me a star."

" 'Just come with me to New York,' he said. 'I'll take care of the rest,' he said.

"I told him I had to check with my mom. I told him I was afraid because I didn't have any money.

" 'You do that,' he said. 'Here's my card,' he said.

"My mom and I checked everything out. He had a big office in New York, and everything seemed on the up & up. So, I begged my mom to let me go. I told her it would be OK. Slim talked to her on the phone and promised to take care of everything. So, I got on a bus, and went to meet him."

Cindy looked at me and shook her head slowly, trying to pull off a smile. She kept trying to shape her mouth into something that looked like a smile, but the anger and embarrassment and hurt kept pouring out instead.

"As soon as I got to the city, and met him at a hotel, Slim seemed different. 'We're not going to be doing any music videos today,' he told me. He was kind of laughing this really sickening laugh. I told him I wanted to get out. I was crying.

"He made me have sex with him. And then he threw me into a room with three other girls and locked the door.

" 'I'm a little short of cash today, girls,' he told us. 'I need you to go out and earn your keep before I can make you a star,' he said. So he forced all of us to get dressed in these cheap clothes, and to work the streets."

"He wanted you to be a prostitute the first night," I said.

"Yes," she said. "He told me he owned me now," she said. "He said to 'get out there and earn some money before I hurt you.'

"I was scared to death, but I decided to act real cool,

and pretend I'd do what he said. I got dressed up, and began to walk the streets with the other girls. He was watching us like a hawk, except for a minute. That's when I ran.

"I ran to a pay phone around the corner, and called the police. They said they'd be there in a second. But Slim saw me. He ran over to me and started beating me, until he heard the siren. Then he ran."

When the police got to Cindy's side, she was spread out on the pavement, bleeding from the lip, with contusions over her body. In the ambulance, on the way to the hospital, Cindy kept saying one thing over and over again. "I want to get that guy," she said. "I want to get that guy."

That night, the moment the doctors were finished bandaging her up, Cindy pressed charges. The next morning, the police arrested Slim, and brought Cindy to Covenant House, so she'd have a safe place to stay before she went to court.

(Sometimes the police use Covenant House as a safe haven for kids in cases like these. The sex industry is a savage 'business,' run by vile and filthy people who will stop at nothing to hurt, and yes kill, kids like Cindy who choose to turn against it. There is no 'secret' hideaway that can safely shield children from the long and vicious arm of these people. Children like Cindy are murdered just to make a point! Given this reality, we've frequently worked with the police to provide round-the-clock safety for kids like Cindy....)

On the morning of the trial, a police escort pulled

up to Covenant House, and drove Cindy and me to court. When we got inside, Slim was sitting at his table, neatly book-ended by two lawyers dressed in $1,000 pinstriped suits, smiling to himself. I had to mentally scrub my mouth out with soap just looking at him. I made a half-hearted apology to God for hating him as much as I did, gave Cindy a hug and sat down.

The trial was everything you'd expect, and dread, in a 1995 court case. Slim's defense lawyers spoke passionately about their client's outstanding record in the community, his impeccable standing in the music industry, his frequent gifts to charity.

"This girl is simply angry she didn't get a role in one of our client's videos, your honor," the lawyers said with conviction. "We are outraged she would impugn our client's integrity with this story." Through it all, they made it clear that Slim was the victim and that Cindy was the one who should really be on trial.

When it got to be Cindy's turn, she detailed her story with a calmness and resoluteness that almost brought tears to my eyes. Even under the awesome onslaught of cross-examination, she never wavered, peering directly at Slim as she spoke.

"He forced me to have sex with him," she said. "He locked me up, and then tried to make me prostitute for him," she said. "He beat me when I tried to run away," she said.

For their part, New York's finest told the court of the rescue at the pay phone, pointing a telling finger at the esteemed defendant. As the trial wore on, Slim's smirk began to fade, replaced by panic.

When it was over, the verdict was loud and clear. Slim was found guilty of assault, sex with a minor and trafficking in prostitution. It's not clear yet exactly how much time he'll get, but God knows he will have 'earned' every single day of his sentence. I hope the judge throws the book at him.

As for Cindy? Earlier this morning, I took her to the airport, where she flew home to meet her mother, and put this incredibly painful chapter behind her (by the way, during her stay at Covenant House, Cindy kept in daily contact with her mom over the phone, assuring her she was OK, while politely refusing to 'drop this whole thing' and come home. "This guy messed with the wrong person," Cindy kept saying over the phone. "I'm not going to let him do that to someone else.")

"Thank you, Sister, for helping me do this," she said as we hugged in the airport. "I'm the one who should thank you," I said. "I'm so proud of you," I said. "Thanks," she said. "It was nothing," she said.

As she got on that plane, and turned around to wave, I felt like crying and cheering at the same time. I know I'll never, ever forget her, and I give thanks to God for bringing her to us.

We won a big one this month. We really did. Thanks to a very good and very courageous kid, one less evil and vile pimp will be roaming our streets tonight.

And maybe you and I proved something too, didn't we? I think the toughest part of being an adult today is not so much the feeling that we have almost lost the ability to protect our children — *but the fear that many of us have lost the will to do so.* It's not easy to be a rabble-rouser nowadays, to fight the lawyers in $1,000 suits, the pervasive leniency, the frustration and fatigue. Cindy, though, showed us once again that she had the will to fight for what's good and right. And through your constant prayers and support of our kids, you've repeatedly demonstrated that will too.

I'm sure that as God looks down on His world, He must be extra proud of Cindy and you today. I know — I just know — He is really thankful for what Cindy did, and the helping hand you gave her.

Learn to Listen

Learn to listen like a teddy bear,
With ears open and mouth closed tight.
Learn to forgive like a teddy bear,
With an open heart, not caring who is right.
Learn to love like a teddy bear,
With arms open and imperfect eyesight.
Do not ask for your life's load lightened,
But for courage to endure.
Do not ask for fulfillment in all your life,
Do not ask for perfection in all you do,
But for the wisdom not to repeat mistakes.
And finally, do not ask for more,
Before saying, "Thank you,"
For what you have already received.
If you're looking for somebody to blame —
Look in the mirror.
There is no challenge that cannot be met,
And dream that cannot be achieved.

*Written by one of our
Covenant House kids*

Chapter 12

"Every time they got drunk
I got beaten...."

"I just want to sleep," he said.

"Please, let me sleep."

He stood outside our doorway, a little boy, propped on each side by two other homeless kids.

His left eye was so swollen and black and blue, he couldn't see a thing out of it.

His eyes dripped tears like faucets.

He was nine, maybe ten, years old.

For three days he wouldn't tell us who he was. "I just want to sleep," was all he said. "I just want to sleep."

We thought maybe he had been in a street fight. But after three days he finally began to trust us enough to tell us what had happened.

He had been beaten by both his parents at once.

Ten years old — one eye swollen — black and blue — cuts all over.

Andrew had run away from home.

"My mother and father ... they always beat me up," he finally told me. "Every time they got drunk, I got beaten up. I couldn't live there anymore, I just couldn't.

"So I ran away. I had to."

He was four foot six inches tall, with dirty brown hair and eyes to match, sixty-two pounds soaking wet ... and he was totally, completely alone.

"I was so scared after I ran ... I just didn't know what to do, Sister. I had some money I had saved up ... so I took a bus from my house on Long Island.

"I ended up just wandering around on the streets ... I didn't know where to go. Then I met those big kids who brought me here. They said maybe you could help me?"

Andrew stopped, and then looked up at me. I've never seen two lonelier eyes in my life. They lingered there for eight, ten seconds, getting heavier and heavier with each passing moment. It seemed like he was carrying the entire weight of the world in those eyes. Finally, though, it got to be too much. The floodgates began to open. Andrew just put his head down, and cried.

I had to take a quiet deep breath or I would have started crying, too.

"I'm so sorry, Andrew. I know how hurt you must be ... how painful it must be. We all feel so lucky you found us ... we're really glad you came to us."

"Those big kids were right, Andrew. We do want to help you.

"We really want to help you. Will you let us?"

He looked up at me, biting his lips as hard as he could, trying to stop the tears for a minute. Then, his head started bobbing up and down, first slowly, then faster and faster. I could tell he really liked the idea a lot.

"OK, Sister," he finally said. "OK."

"Thanks, Andrew," I said and I gave him a big hug. "Thanks for letting us be your friend."

"Thank you."

This entire conversation took place about three and a half hours ago. As I write you this letter, I have no idea what's going to happen, long-term, to this beautiful — and very courageous! — little boy.

I wish I had a better answer than that. But right now I don't.

I feel very strongly that Andrew should not go back to his parents unless they get professional help. No way! This little boy should not suffer this way ever again.

As for what will happen to Andrew while he is with us, I can tell you this. We will love him and care for him. Every moment he is at Covenant House, he will know from us that he is special, and worthy and loved.

Every single child — every child! — deserves to know that he or she is loved.

Andrew has probably never known that feeling.

But he will. I promise you he will.

Chapter 13

"I really would rather rot out here than go back to them."

"My name is David," he whispered that first night we met him. "I don't want to be out here on the street," he said. "I'm afraid I'm going to die," he said.

"But I'd rather die out here on the street, than try to live at home," he said.

He was a little scrawny kid, the tiniest child we'd ever seen from our van. His hands and feet were so small, his features so frail, that he looked like a little mouse under the flickering light of the street lamp. He was the sweetest-looking street kid we've ever met....

"Please don't ask me to come back to your shelter," he told us that first night. "I can't," he said. "I'm sorry," he said. And then he crept off into the darkness.

The second time we met him was a drizzly night two weeks ago, under the same flickering street lamp. We'd been out in the van, looking for him....

"I guess you're wondering why I'm here," he said that night. "I don't have a choice," he said. "My stepfather ... my stepfather is a pervert ... he beats me and does sexual stuff to me, too. Ever since I was 12 (David is 14), he's been getting into bed with me.

"I reported him to the counselors at school, but my stepfather denied it, and my mom got mad at me. He just kept doing it. And...."

My little friend couldn't finish his story that night. The tears made sure he couldn't....

"We'd like to be your friend. Please come back with us ... we can help you."

"I can't," he said. "I gotta keep running." And he did just that, running away down an alley. We tried calling out to him, but he kept running....

Earlier tonight, because he was so hungry his stomach hurt and so drenched from the rain he needed dry clothes, David dropped by our shelter for a minute.

"I can't stay," he announced the second he walked in. "I gotta go ... gotta keep moving."

As soon as I heard he was here, I raced downstairs to meet him. I was able to catch up, just as he was leaving the building....

"I've been looking for you, David. We all have."

"I know," the little mouse said. "I've been hiding, I've been moving," he said. "Kids like me don't have no choice. We gotta keep moving. I got to go, Sister."

"Please talk to me," I said. "I want to help you."

"No one can help me," he said. He backed up against our brick building as he spoke so he could lean against it. He felt more comfortable that way, more in control, more able to scan the dark streets that run alongside. Like everything else he did, he did it for a reason.

"Why don't you come inside the cafeteria again with me. For a second. We'll pack you a few more sandwiches for the night."

"I can't do that," he said. "I gotta stand here. No offense, but this way I can see you and everyone else. I gotta make sure no one sneaks up behind me. They're after me," he said.

"Who's after you?"

"Everyone," he said.

"I mean, my stepfather and mother want me back. They say it doesn't 'look good' to be running away. So they got the police to search for me.

"I won't let them get me, Sister," he said. "I really would rather rot out here than go back to them," he said.

"Then stay with us," I said. "We'll help you."

"I can't," the mouse said, shaking his head. "I know the rules," he said.

"If I stay with you, you'll have to tell my parents you found me," he said. "I'd rather die," he said.

Tears formed in his eyes as he talked. There was nothing — absolutely nothing — cynical or mean-spirited or chippy about the way he talked. Even though he was just a little kid, he had learned all the rules on the street. From a purely legal standpoint, he *was* right. If he stayed in our shelter, we *would* have to report that to the authorities.

"Maybe we can work out something better," I said. "Please give us a try," I said. "We can help ... maybe we can work out a plan so you can live with another relative. You've got to get off the street, David, before it kills you. We'll do all we can to help you, I promise," I said.

"But first you've got to get off the streets before

something really bad happens."

"Something bad has," he said. "It already has." The tears were beginning to gush out now. I put my hand on his shoulder. He started to turn away, but then froze. He didn't want me to let go.

"It's not my fault, Sister," he sniffled. "But I've got hooked up with some people who aren't that good. I mean, at least they give me a place to stay," he said. "And they give me money for all the stuff I have to do," he said. I knew what the "stuff" was that he was talking about.

"I know it's not your fault, David," I said. "You're a really good person," I said. "But these people ... your pimp ... they're not good, David. They're not good for you," I said.

"I mean, these people are very, very dangerous. And there are too many bad things that can happen to you," I said. "Things like AIDS," I said.

(The idea that I was speaking to an innocent, sweet, sobbing 14-year-old kid about AIDS in the middle of the night made my heart ache. I honestly thought I was going to get ill at that moment. Please help me keep it together, God, I prayed to myself.)

"I can't worry about AIDS," David mumbled softly to the street pavement. "I'm probably going to die anyway," he said. "What difference does it make how it happens?"

He put his hand on my hand, which was still resting on his shoulder, and tried to smile. For a few seconds, we just looked at each other, doing all we could to let the other person know we cared, both of us knowing he'd be gone in a second.

"I gotta go," he finally said. "I'm sorry ... I really wish I didn't have to go," he said. "My pimp is probably mad as it is," he said.

"Stay with us," I tried one last time.

"Maybe next time," he said. "I'll think about it," he said.

"Thanks," he said.

"Don't give up on yourself," I yelled out loud. "Don't give up on him, God," I whispered, knowing that He hadn't.

"I'm never giving up on you, David," I said.

Chapter 14

"I want to go back where I belong."

The other kids called her "The Girl in the Hood."

She came to our shelter one frigid night, a very large and unsure girl wearing a huge red hood pulled over her head.

From the second she stepped inside, she cast a shadow over our shelter — a shadow that was bigger and shrouded in more mystery than any other kid I have ever met.

"Who is that girl in the hood, anyway," the kids would whisper. "What does she look like under that hood? Does she ever take it off? *Ever?*"

"She just needs some space," I told them. "Please give her time."

For her first 30 days at Covenant House, *she never once took her hood off*, never once showed her eyes. She wore the hood every minute in the morning, and every minute throughout the day. She even wore her hood to bed at night, pulling it tightly over her eyes as she drifted off to sleep.

All our cajoling and pleading and counseling couldn't get her to take it off. She wouldn't — she couldn't — give away the one thing in life that helped her hide.

The kids found her ... unnerving. Hard to understand. A little scary. Even the toughest, street-hardened, seen-it-all-and-had-it-all-done-to-them kids kept a safe distance away.

From the beginning we decided to be extra patient with her, to give her as much space as we could. But always, always, we were there, too. Because she obviously needed us there more than any other kid I ever met....

Our conversations (and we never stopped trying to start one) weren't much longer than a hiccup those first weeks. "Hi," I'd say. "Hi," she'd say. "I'd love to talk to you when you get a chance," I'd say. "OK," she'd say, as she walked away.

Many times, while she was all alone at a table by herself, I'd drop by to say hello and pat her on the back. "I'd love to talk to you when you're ready," I'd say. "OK," her hood would nod. "Later," she'd say.

For a month this went on, little snippets of conversation here, a nod there. Her words, so few spoken over those 30 days, always came the same way, barely a whisper, head and eyes down, escaping under the cover of her hood.

We learned that her name was Nancy. She was a runaway from North Carolina. She had been severely abused at home, by both her parents, and was so terrified she bought a bus ticket (with the only money she had) and escaped to New York. She ended up at the Port Authority, all alone, and wandered the streets for weeks ... until a kind policeman brought her to us. She was scared. And hurt. And no one cared about her. No one.

"No one wants me," she said one night out of the blue while she was getting up from dinner. She never looked up when she said it. At that moment, it was more clear than ever why Nancy hid inside her hood. I mean, her hood was much more than an article of clothing for Nancy. It was her cocoon ... her sanctuary, the only safe and secure place that was hers and hers alone.

By hiding beneath her hood, Nancy was able to hide the incredible feelings of insecurity that paralyzed her. Her hood became her "alter ego" — her protector (the only protector she knew). Her round-the-clock security blanket. The only place in the world she felt safe.

Finally, though, our love got through to her....

"I was wondering, Nancy," I said again one day. "We really think it's time we get you some new clothes. I'd really like to buy you a new dress to wear." (It was probably the 99th time I suggested it — I wasn't really expecting much.)

The hood slowly lifted, and her eyes met mine (it was only for a split second, but it was a first). "Really?" she said. After we got her a new outfit, I brought her up to Billie, one of our super counselors who ironically had also been a hairdresser. "Will you let Billie do your hair, Nancy?" I asked. "You'd look so nice."

"I don't know," she said. "I'm so ugly," she said. "Everyone thinks I am," she said. For the first time, I could see tears streaming down her face.

"Please let us," I said. "You'll look terrific," I said, putting my hand on her hood, and gently pulling it back.

It was difficult keeping our composure those next few moments, seeing and feeling and touching and smelling hair that had been matted down for months. Our new scissors almost failed, her hair was so stiff.

"Please stop ... maybe this isn't a good idea," she kept saying. "I'm so ugly ... don't waste your time."

"You look great," we said. "You really do."

During the next week, a very scared and unsure kid didn't leave her room that much. Every night, around 5:45, I'd see her make a quick beeline to the cafeteria, eyes straight down, and then back to her room 30 minutes later.

"Hi Nancy, it's great to see you today. You look wonderful," I would always tell her. "Thanks," she would mumble.

But as time wore on, Nancy ventured out of her room more often. Slowly, she began to talk to the other kids. To smile, and even to laugh. Her counseling sessions, once frustratingly short, became longer. The pain and anger she had literally wrapped inside her, began to flow out.

It wasn't an overnight transformation. There were days when Nancy slipped back into her own little world. But slowly, surely, she began to blossom under the light of our love, a beautiful child of God discovering an internal beauty she had never known.

She was literally reborn.

Then last week, she surprised us all. "I want to go back to North Carolina," she said. "To live near my old home. I've got a cousin who says I can live with her.

She's a good person. I want to go back where I belong."

A few hours ago, I picked up the phone to hear a cheerful voice calling from North Carolina. "It's working out great, Sister," she said. "I just got a job today," she said. "It doesn't pay much, but it's a start. Thanks ... thanks," she said.

"I'm so happy," I said.

"Thank you, thank you," she said. The voice was filled with tears, but I never heard one so beautiful.

Chapter 15

"I'm going to be a nurse,"
she declared. "I'm going to make it."
I'm sure she is.

Fourteen-year-old Brian frantically dialed our NINELINE crisis hotline Tuesday night, from a deserted payphone in Los Angeles. "I want to get out of this gang I'm in," he cried. "But I don't know how. The last kid who tried to leave was stabbed in the eye," he said.

Our NINELINE staff immediately hooked Brian up with two gang intervention services in his area, and led him to safety. *He's safe at home now....*

Thirteen-year-old Kelly called Tuesday night too, scared out of her mind. "My stepfather is abusing me," she told our NINELINE volunteers. "He's ... he's doing stuff to me at night." Our NINELINE team helped Kelly report her sexual abuse to her state's welfare agency, who arranged for a protective services worker to meet Kelly at the local police department.

Today Kelly is safe, living with her mother in another state....

Jackie called two nights ago from another pay phone in a dark city alley, fear quivering from her voice. "I ran away from my mom two days ago," the 15-year-old told our counselors. "I feel so stupid ... I'm so

scared ... I need help ... I'm afraid I'm going to die."
Within ten minutes we helped reconcile Jackie with her
mother, over a three-way phone hook up.

Today, Jackie is safely at home, another kid rescued
in the nick of time from the street....

Jose knows what it's like to be saved by your love
too. Two weeks ago, his alcoholic father kicked 16-
year-old Jose out of his house and left this crippled kid
alone on the street (Jose doesn't have a mother — she
died years ago). "I didn't have a place to go ... I just
slept on subways ... I ate food off the street," Jose told
us. "Then someone told me there was a place called
Covenant House where people care."

Today Jose is safe and sound, and a prime candidate
for our Rights of Passage program....

Kimberly knows all about pain and fighting back
too. At the age of 13, Kim was raped in a deserted
schoolyard in one of the toughest sections of a big mid-
western city. When it happened again 18 months later,
Kim's alcoholic mother kicked her out of the house.
"It's your fault," she said. "You're no good. You're
going to be a failure just like me."

When Kim finally found Covenant House nine
months ago, she looked three times older than her 15
years. But through hard work, lots of counseling, and
tons of love, Kim has begun to reclaim her life. "I'm
going to be a nurse," she declared the day she enrolled
in our educational vocational program. "I'm going to
make it." I'm sure she is....

Fourteen-year-old Mandy found her personal

rebirth here this week too. Three weeks ago this scared and incredibly tiny girl had fled her single father in Connecticut who "didn't have time for me anymore," and ran away with a 22-year-old boy. Since then, she had been living in the back of an abandoned restaurant in Florida — without running water and with the agony of being abused and beaten every night.

Finally, last week Mandy worked up the courage to phone the police who rushed to her "home," forcibly removed her from the clutches of her boyfriend, and brought her to Covenant House. Our counselors helped Mandy contact her deliriously relieved father, and arranged for Mandy to return home, another urban nomad rescued from an inevitably grotesque ending on the street.

Kathy knows all about living and dying too. Nine and a half months ago, this sixteen-year-old "made a terrible mistake" and got pregnant. "I didn't think for a minute about giving up my baby," she said. "I knew I had to have him." Unfortunately, her father couldn't see beyond his anger, and threw Kathy and her baby out on the street the moment they came back from the hospital.

Two weeks ago Kathy began going to school in our Rights of Passage program (she was an honor student in school) with dreams of becoming a nurse. With our help, she's already set up special day care arrangements, and has begun working at a job too. "Me and my baby are going to make it," she says proudly. There's not a question in my mind she will....

Frankie knows what it's like to find help and salvation here too. Five years ago, he immigrated from a Central American country, leaving behind seven brothers and sisters and two parents who told him, "We can't feed you any more." Frankie had everything in the world going against him — he couldn't speak English, he didn't know a soul, he was absolutely petrified how he would survive. But he did have Covenant House and you.

Last week, five years after coming to Covenant House with nothing and going through our Rights of Passage program, Frankie came back to us carrying a bouquet of roses and a note for his teacher, Sally. "Thanks for everything," the note said. "I couldn't have made it without Covenant House," it said. "God bless you greatly."

The card also contained a gift from Frankie — a $100 check which he's asked us to use "to help other kids."

Brian.

Kelly.

Jackie.

Jose.

Kimberly.

Mandy.

Kathy.

Frankie.

Eight frantic kids. Eight hopeless situations. Eight kids delivered from their own private infernos, their own living and breathing Hell. It's been another good week for resurrections here at Covenant House.

It's kind of ironic these kids teach us so much. I mean, there's nothing the 'rest of the world' would say is "special" about these kids. They are scared, sometimes impetuous, often angry, frequently dirty, all-too-often faceless and nameless kids who have fallen through (or been pushed through) the delicate cracks which underpin our society.

None of these kids set out in life to seek us, or seek the situation in which they live. Each of these kids called us, or fled to us or was led to us for one simple and very unromantic reason — they had no where else to go.

I'm sure none of them see themselves as God's presents to us. If I suggested that to them, they'd look at me like I had two heads. But they are. The Resurrection happening inside each of them — their transformation from a lifetime of pain to a today filled with hope — is visible in every one of their eyes.

Maybe that's the greatest gift all of us can learn from Covenant House. That in giving of ourselves to Covenant House, He has allowed us to be 1996 witnesses to Resurrection each and every day. Even if these kids can't see it inside themselves!

It's one of the most beautiful things I have ever seen.

Chapter 16

"I made this promise to God...."

NUN FOR HIRE

Catholic nun looking for a chance to speak at churches and civic groups about God's kids. Great stories of kids in seemingly hopeless situations, desperate escapes, daring rescues, heartwarming love, happy endings.

No salary requested! (But I would like the chance to ask for donations to help homeless kids!)

If interested, write to: Sister Mary Rose, Covenant House, 346 West 17th Street, New York, NY 10011. An Equal Denominational Speaker.

Do you belong to a church group that might be willing to listen to this nun for a few minutes? Maybe a PTA? I'd love the chance to tell you about our beautiful kids. I've got some really incredible, heartwarming stories to share. (You'd be surprised how many kids come from your neck of the woods!)

Please let me know, if you can. I've made a promise to God that I'm going to talk to anyone and everyone who'll listen, to tell them about our homeless kids

... and beg for their help.

Ever since God put me in this new position as President of Covenant House (I'm convinced He arranged the whole thing), I've been looking for ways to get the word out about our kids.

Give me a call. I've got some really great things to tell your friends.

Epilogue

On this early June evening, I'm looking out my window onto a glorious sunset. The record-breaking winter of 1995 – 96 is behind us, and the blistering heat of summer is on its way. At this moment, looking west into God's beautiful creation, it's hard to imagine that the streets below could be filled with anything but love and joy for our children.

In my own childhood, this was the kind of gentle evening perfect for sitting on a stoop with a friend and an ice cream cone.

But the world is a very different place for children these days — and I fear it will only get worse.

Just moments ago, I stood on the stoop of Covenant House as kids began arriving, seeking refuge from the dangers of the street.

Tonight, tomorrow morning and in the days to come, our counselors and I will hear their sad, and terrible and still-untold stories.

Tonight we'll shelter more boys like 10-year-old Andrew, who will come to our shelter carrying black and blue marks on the outside which pale in comparison to the hurt and pain they feel in their hearts.

Tonight we'll welcome more girls like Janice, innocent waifs who have been pulled into a savage world of prostitution and pain, and yearn to escape before they are forced to "work" one more night on our streets.

We'll hand out towels and clean clothes to more Melissas, more Davids, more Lizs....

In short, we'll share our Covenant with more than one thousand kids this night ...

... each kid asking silently, "Are you out there, God?"

Will you help me answer?

Your prayers and your love for these lost children ... and your financial support of our Covenant — that we will turn no child away — will help me answer in His Name: "Yes, my beloved child. Yes! I am out here. And I am with you!"

Thank you for reading our kids' stories. Thank you for taking the time to read about our work. And if you can, please join us in our lifesaving mission. The need grows more urgent every day. Thank you, and God bless you.

In His love,

Sister Mary Rose McGeady
For the kids

*"I bound myself by oath,
I made a covenant with you ...
and you became mine."*

Ezekiel 16:8

*(Our oath, the first thing kids see
when they walk into our shelter.)*

A Call to Faith

A Letter from a Covenant House Community member

I don't remember exactly what possessed me the evening I decided to do some sort of volunteer work. I will never forget driving to a Cleveland Cavaliers game with my parents, announcing from the backseat, "I think I'm going to sell my business and go do some missionary work." An announcement like this took everyone by surprise, especially my brother who didn't hesitate to ask if I was feeling okay.

At the time, I was the owner of a very successful Subway Sandwich Shop. To those people around me everything seemed perfect, but I knew inside something wasn't quite right. I kept feeling there was something else I was supposed to be doing and somehow on the way to the basketball game it all clicked. All of a sudden I felt a deep burning need to help others who hadn't been as fortunate as myself.

I was getting real comfortable with the idea. I started reviewing my options and decided that Covenant House Faith Community was the place for me. When I read the basic requirements I began to wonder if my brother wasn't right and that maybe I did need my head examined. What was it that was making me want to leave my extremely comfortable lifestyle to pray twice a day, work with street kids, live communally with a bunch of strangers and make $15 a week? At the time I couldn't grasp exactly what it was but I knew one thing for sure, that I had to go check this place out.

I flew to New York City to stay with the Faith Community for a week. It was one of the most confusing weeks of my life. I had so many questions to ask and they had some for me as well. I started the week knowing this was the place for me and by the time Friday came I was ready to go home and considering volunteering somewhere else. At the end of the week I was advised to go home, relax and pray for help with my decision.

I took the advice I had been given to heart. I was so confused and I knew God was the only one that could show me the path I was to take next. I relaxed and prayed for a sign. Unfortunately, no sign dropped from the sky telling me what to do, nor did the voice of God speak to me, but gradually an unbelievable peace came over me and I knew Covenant House Faith Community was the place for me. Somehow everything was going to be okay.

It's hard for me to believe I'm getting near the end of my 13-month commitment. I've learned so much about myself, the kids and God. I've learned, for instance, that sometimes it's our own insecurities that keep us from drawing closer and listening to others. Street kids, I've come to learn, have a lot more to offer me about life than I could ever hope to teach them.

I've also come to see that God moves in truly mysterious ways. Whenever I've looked to God in desperation, somehow, I've always come out of the experience with peace of mind.

I don't know yet what I will be doing at the end of my commitment, but I do know a few things for sure. For instance, I made the right decision when I joined Faith Community; God was calling me closer and I responded. It's scary not being sure of my next move, but I know that when the time comes to make that decision God will give me the gentle assurance I need. Surely, I will find compassion in my heart every time I see a homeless person. Lastly, and perhaps more importantly, I know that street kids can appear rough and undeserving, but just like you and I, they deserve to be treated with respect and love.

"Dear Covenant House..."

A former kid ... 15 years later

Dear Covenant House:

Hello, my name is JoAnn (▮▮▮▮▮▮▮▮▮▮. I've been in Covenant House when it first opened back in the late 70's. At that time is was called "UNDER 21."

I had the best Social Worker a HURT, LOST, and LONELY teenager could have, her name is "Laura ▮▮▮▮."

Laura helped me get past my Father's death and my mother's everyday mental and physical abuse to me. If it wasn't for Covenant House-Under 21, I probably wouldn't be here today.

At the time I was at Under 21, I was 18 years old, now I'm 34 years old and I live in Washington, D.C. I work for ▮▮▮▮▮▮▮▮, ▮▮▮▮▮▮▮▮▮▮▮." I'm the Administrative Secretary for "▮▮▮▮▮▮▮▮▮▮▮▮▮▮▮▮▮▮▮."

Anyway, when I went to Under 21, I was 18 yrs. old and had no place to go, my mother didn't want me, and my father just passed away. *I wasn't scared of the streets, I was tired of running them with no place to lay my head.* Covenant House-Under 21, took me in, fed me, and gave me hope. They helped me get on Public Assistance, which in turn gave me a place of my own (a room), and from there I went back to school for typing, and eventually I got my first full time job working in an insurance company, and I have been moving up from that point on. *Thanks to the help of Under 21.*

It's funny, 17 years ago I was living at Covenant House and here it is today, 4/5/95, 17 years later, I'm reading one of your books "Am I Going To Heaven," and it took me back to the days of Under 21.

All I can say on paper is: Please continue helping the kids that show up at your door, a lot of us aren't really bad, we have no one to turn to, and a lot of times, we have no one to talk to and *Covenant House does make a difference.*

If at all possible, I would like to come to Covenant House and speak to the young adults that come there, and the ones that stay there. I believe in sharing my success, especially considering one of them is now using the space I once occupied. This is how I can give something back from what I learned!!

                              God Bless,
                              Joanne ▮▮▮▮▮▮▮

Where do we go from here?

My newsletters tell an incredible story ... but they only tell part of the story. Wrapped around the letters I wrote to my friends, I've also included words written to me by others — poems and prayers written by our kids, and letters sent to me by donors who were moved by what they see happening in America today.

And almost every word in this book — whether they were penned by me, a runaway kid, a nervous grandmother, or a teenager in school — carries a consistent message: the American family is falling apart. And we must, each of us, do what we can to repair it. Now!

I passionately believe the breakdown of the family unit is the single deepest ethical and moral challenge of our generation. Whether we respond to it will depend on the resolve and willingness of all of us to commit ourselves to the care and protection of family life. The time for repairing endangered families and rescuing their children is not after they have fallen apart!

The question then is ... how? How can each of us make a difference in repairing the American family? And how can we begin to make that difference now?

Because the survival of the family is so very important to our futures, we have prepared a special Family Survival Guide which can be found on the fol-

lowing pages. This Guide features the best things
we've learned over the years working with hundreds of
thousands of kids, as well as good, time-tested values
that we never let ourselves forget. We hope you will
share these pages with a parent you know who may
need help. Thank you!

Family
Survival
Guide

Reflections on
Raising Kids Today

Values – Teaching Them in Today's World.

Communicating your values has never been more important than it is today. And the good news is, it all begins and ends with you.

When all is said and done, parents have far more influence over instilling values in their kids than any other factor.

Here are some simple, and very important, things we should all remember about values, and passing them along:

• Kids get their sense of what's right and wrong from people they love and respect. No one has more influence over teaching values than you do. Your input can make all the difference!

• When it comes to teaching values .... action *always* speaks louder than words. Kids today have a "show me" mentality. They need to see the values lived out by you. Respect for life, respect for other people, honesty, integrity ... kids get those from watching you. The old saw has never been more true ... children *do* learn what they live!

• Families are still the best vehicle for raising children. A loving, nurturing family unit, of whatever form, creates the kind of environment kids need to learn what's right and wrong ... and how to love themselves too. Values are best inculcated in an environment of love and acceptance.

• Always take time to sit and talk to your kids. Don't be afraid to say what you feel (but don't ever be too closed to listen to what your kids think).

- Always strive to teach your kids to love and respect themselves as children of God. A healthy love and respect for themselves is incredibly important for any kid. It's also the first essential step in helping a kid also learn a love and respect for those around him, and God.

- Nobody has said it better than Jesus. Those three words, "Love Thy Neighbor...." are an important message for every kid!

You've Got a Tough Job.

Most of us were never taught to be parents. So we can't help but disappoint ourselves sometimes. How often have you heard yourself using the very words you hated hearing from your own parents?

And when our kids become teenagers, it gets even harder. They seem to reject everything we've taught them. As far as they're concerned, we know nothing. Our values and beliefs are constantly challenged. Every word we utter is seen as interference. Emotions run high.

But we're more important to our teens than ever. As they try out the values of their peers, who are more influential than ever, we counter the pull of drugs and alcohol. These entangle children every day and can ruin their lives.

The Stakes Are High.

Teenagers who don't get what they need at home look elsewhere. Some run away from home. Many more consider other ways of running from pressure — a once bright and happy son escapes to drugs, a vivacious daughter starts drinking. Think about these facts:

- Each year, one million students drop out of high school or are chronically truant.
- Four out of 10 teenage girls will become pregnant before age 20.
- Although marijuana use has declined in the past years, addiction to cocaine, especially crack, has doubled.
- One in four teens develops a drinking problem during his teen years; about 10,000 will die in alcohol-related accidents this year.
- Each year, 5,000 to 6,000 teens die in suicide-related deaths, and the number is growing, one every 90 minutes. For every death, at least 100 other young people attempt suicide.

The Turbulent Teens.

Teens face many pressures that adults don't take seriously. Their bodies are changing — they have to adjust to the new person they see in the mirror. They feel different. They become interested in sex.

Self-doubt is constant. They feel pressure to conform and fear ridicule if they don't.

These changes can be bewildering, frightening and even depressing.

Teens can have remarkable insights. But they also surprise us with their lack of good judgment.

Your Teen Needs You.

At the time teenagers are crying out to be treated as adults, they also need a nurturing home, a refuge. And though they deny it passionately, they need structure, limits, lots of help sorting out their lives and most important, love.

In the turbulence of growing up, it is important for us parents to remember (even if our teens seem to forget) that we love each other. In the end, that's what makes the whole struggle worthwhile.

How Well Do You Know Your Kids?

You may say, "My teenager wouldn't do that." Most don't. But even if yours wouldn't, think about the following questions:

- Where is your child right now?
- What are your teen's deepest fears?
- Who is your son or daughter's best friend?
- Do your teen's friends feel welcome in your home?

Remember, a strong relationship with your children is the best way for you to guide them, and to prevent them from becoming a sorry statistic.

Getting Along With Your Teen.

Here are some ideas and techniques you can try to improve your relationship with your teen. If they don't work at first, keep trying. They take practice.

1. Make time for your teen. Find an activity you enjoy doing together and pursue it. If your invitations are declined, keep asking.

2. Listen, really listen. Because parents have so much to do and so little time, we often try to listen while cleaning, washing dishes or fixing the car. Put your chores aside so your teen knows you're really paying attention.

3. Take the long view. Don't treat minor mishaps as major catastrophes. Choose the important issues. Don't make your home a battleground.

4. Tolerate differences. View your teenager as an individual distinct from you. This doesn't mean you can't state your opinion if you disagree.

5. Respect your teenager's privacy. If a behavior is worrying you, speak up.

6. Let your teens sort things out themselves. Never say that you know how your teen feels. They believe their feelings (so new and personal) are unique. They'll learn otherwise — without your help. And never imply that their feelings don't matter or will change. Because teens live in the present, it doesn't matter that they'll soon feel differently.

7. Don't judge. State facts instead of opinions when

you praise or criticize. Stating facts like "Your poem made me smile," or "This report card is all Cs and Ds!" leaves it up to your teen to draw the appropriate conclusions. Teens are sensitive about being judged — positively as well as negatively.

8. Be generous with praise. Praise your child's efforts, not just accomplishments. And don't comment on the person. "You're a great artist" is hard to live up to. "I loved that drawing" is a fact and comes from your heart.

9. Set reasonable limits. Teens need them. Your rules should be consistently applied — and rooted in your deepest beliefs and values.

10. Teach your teen to make sensible decisions and choices by encouraging independence and letting your teenager make mistakes. Don't step in unless you have to.

How to Make Anger Work.

All parents get furious at their children. We can't help it. But some parents feel bad about being angry and keep quiet. Though it's easy to say things in anger that you don't mean, anger can also spark talks that will help you and your teen get to know each other better.

Some Guidelines.

• When you get mad, don't blame or accuse. Say how you *feel* — annoyed, irritated, upset, etc. —

and why. Be specific. Talk facts. Blaming only forces a teen to argue his point, arouses tempers, and kills dialogue.

- Think solution, not victory. Don't try to win arguments.

- Stick to the present incident. Fighting old battles will only aggravate a situation.

- Be careful not to attack your teen's person or character. Say, "I'm furious that you didn't clean up after the mess you made" — *not,* "You're a lazy slob!" Your son or daughter may give up trying to improve.

- If the situation is touchy, put your ideas in a letter. You can say exactly what you mean — and your teen will have time to think it over before answering.

Signs That Your Child Needs Outside Help.

- Suicidal talk of any kind. A suicidal teen may also give away valued possessions, make a will, talk about death or dying or say his family would be better off without him.

- Recent changes in sleeping or eating habits, thinking patterns, personality, friendships, study habits, activities. A sudden unexplained end to a long depression often precedes a suicide attempt. Major weight loss can be a sign of bulimia or anorexia — dangerous problems.

- Drug or alcohol use. You might notice: irrational

or irresponsible behavior, lying, secretiveness, severe mood swings, a sudden increase in accidents. A teen with a problem may have dilated pupils or wear sunglasses indoors, or complain about not sleeping or not feeling well. Valuables may disappear. You may find drug paraphernalia or alcohol containers around the house.

- A recent change in friends who you feel may be involved with drugs or alcohol may indicate that your child is involved or be a sign that your child is having other problems.

- Law-breaking behavior, even if the police and courts aren't involved. You might notice new possessions and money not accounted for.

- Poor self-image. Doubts are normal. But persistently low self-esteem is a problem.

- Serious depression. Listlessness, loneliness, withdrawal, difficulty making friends.

- Rebelliousness to the point of total, continual defiance.

- Problems at school, including class-cutting, absenteeism, a sudden drop in grades.

- Fears or anxieties that interfere with everyday activities.

- Problems between family members that aren't solved by listening and discussing. In fact, family changes such as a death, divorce or remarriage are times when teens often need some outside help.

When to Get Help For Yourself.

- Things aren't going well with your family but you can't figure out why.
- You disagree totally with positions your spouse has taken on issues concerning your teen and the two of you can't find a compromise.
- You have trouble holding a job.
- You are abusing drugs or alcohol.
- You get violent with your teenager and can't control yourself.
- Your spouse gets violent with you or your child.

What to Do If Your Teen Runs Away.

Most kids who run away return within 48 hours. Those who stay away can find themselves in many dangerous situations. So do everything you can to bring your child home.

- Keep a notebook recording steps you've taken and dates.
- Check in with: neighbors, relatives, and your teen's friends, teachers, employer or co-workers.
- Contact local hangouts and hospitals.
- Call the police. Have an officer come to your house to take a report and pick up recent photos, dental records and fingerprints if available. Get his name; badge number and phone number; the police report number; and the name of the officer who will follow up.
- Make sure the police lists your teen in the National

Crime Information Center (NCIC) to the state clearinghouse on missing children, if there is one in your state.

- Contact the National Center for Missing and Exploited Children for help with law enforcement officials — 1-800-843-5678.

- Call the Covenant House NINELINE for support and to check for messages. Leave a message. Also check with any local runaway hotlines.

- Contact runaway shelters locally and in nearby states.

- Make posters with photos of your teen, listing: age, height, weight, hair and eye color, complexion, physical characteristics (such as scars, birthmarks, braces or pierced ears), circumstances of disappearance, your phone number and police contacts. Distribute these to truck stops, youth-oriented businesses, hospitals, law-enforcement agencies.

- Be prepared for the first conversation with your teen. Whether in person or by phone, show concern, not anger. Say, "I love you."

- Prepare to quickly begin resolving the problems which caused your child to leave home. When your child returns home, emotions are likely to run high. Someone outside your family can help you all deal with these emotions. You may find that planned time for your teen in a temporary residence or shelter is necessary while you are resolving problems. So get outside help from a trained counselor.

Need expert help or support?

Call our NINELINE counselors at 1-800-999-9999.

We'll put you in touch with people who can help you right in your hometown.

1-800-999-9999

This call is free.

in our educational vocational progr... ...she's going to make it." I'm sure she is....

Fourteen-year-old Mandy folded her personal

Covenant House
346 West 17th Street
New York, NY 10011-5002

Covenant House New Jersey
Atlantic City:
3529 Pacific Avenue
Atlantic City, NJ 08401

Newark:
14 William Street
Newark, NJ 07102

Covenant House Washington, D.C.
P.O. Box 77764
Washington, D.C. 20013

Covenant House Florida
Fort Lauderdale:
733 Breakers Avenue
Fort Lauderdale, FL 33304-4196

Orlando:
888 N. Orange Avenue
Orlando, FL 32801

Covenant House New Orleans
611 North Rampart Street
New Orleans, LA 70112-3540

Covenant House Alaska
609 F Street
Anchorage, AK 99501

Covenant House California
1325 N. Western Avenue
Hollywood, CA 90027-5611

Covenant House Texas
1111 Lovett Boulevard
Houston, TX 77006-3898

Covenant House Donor Assistance Line: 1-800-388-3888
Visit our website at: http://www.Covenant House.org

Are You Out There?

Covenant House depends almost entirely on gifts from friends like you to help 43,000 homeless and run-away children every year. We provide food, clothing, shelter, medical attention, educational and vocational training and counseling to kids with no place to go for help. Please help if you can.

YES! I want to help the kids at Covenant House. Here is my gift of: ☐ **$10** ☐ **$20** ☐ **$25** ☐ **Other**

Name _____

Address _____

City _____ **State** _____ **Zip** _____

Please make your check payable to Covenant House. Your gift is tax deductible.

☐ *Please send me your financial information.*

☐ Please send me _____ copies
of *Are You Out There, God.*

Many people like to charge their gift. If you would like to, please fill out the information below:
I prefer to charge my: ☐ MasterCard ☐ Discover ☐ Visa

Account # _____

Amount _____ **Exp. Date** _____

Signature _____

Mail to:　Covenant House
　　　　　　JAF Box 2973
　　　　　　New York, NY 10116-2973

Or, call 1-800-388-3888 to charge your gift on your
MasterCard, Discover or Visa.　　　COUPON

Copies of our financial and operating reports have been filed with the state and are available on request. To obtain one, simply write: New York State Department of State, Charities Registration Section, 162 Washington Avenue, Albany, NY 12231 or Covenant House, JAF Box 2973, New York, NY 10116-2973.

West Virginia residents may obtain a summary of the registration and financial documents from the Secretary of State, State Capitol, Charleston, WV 25305. Registration does not imply endorsement.

A copy of the official registration and financial information may be obtained from the Pennsylvania Department of State by calling, toll free, within Pennsylvania, 1-800-732-0999. Registration does not imply endorsement.

Registration and financial documents are available from the Maryland Secretary of State, State House, Annapolis, MD 21401. Registration does not imply endorsement.

Covenant House is a member of America's
Charities, a nonprofit federation that represents a
variety of national charities in workplace giving
campaigns. To find out if your employer is a part of
America's Charities call us at: (800) 458-9505.